MW01222547

Pothead's Little Instruction Book

First published 2003 by Boxtree
an imprint of Pan Macmillan Ltd
Pan Macmillan, 20 New Wharf Road, London N1 9RR
Basingstoke and Oxford
Associated companies throughout the world
www.panmacmillan.com

ISBN 0 7522 1568 X

Copyright © Mike Anderiesz 2003

The right of Mike Anderiesz to be identified as the author of
this work has been asserted by him in accordance with the
Copyright, Designs and Patents Act 1988.

All rights reserved. No part of this publication may be
reproduced, stored in or introduced into a retrieval system, or
transmitted, in any form, or by any means (electronic,
mechanical, photocopying, recording or otherwise) without
the prior written permission of the publisher. Any person who
does any unauthorized act in relation to this publication may
be liable to criminal prosecution and civil claims for
damages.

9 8 7 6 5 4 3 2 1

A CIP catalogue record for this book is available from
the British Library.

Typeset by Perfect Bound Ltd
Printed by the Bath Press Ltd

The
POTHEAD'S
Little
INSTRUCTION
BOOK

Dr V. S. Ganjabhang

BOXTREE

Contents

Introduction

Back in 2001, I wrote The Little Book of Pot, *a seminal title that sold over 60,000 copies – not counting the other 60k either stolen or eaten straight off the shelf by munchie-crazed potheads.*

The book changed my life.

Prior to this I was a qualified doctor (well, qualified to drive a fork-lift truck) intent on retiring to my hash plantation to smoke away the profits.

However, those plans were changed in early 2002 when the UK government decided to downgrade the legal status of cannabis. Insiders expect this relaxation will mark a quantum shift in our attitude to so-called soft drugs. For example, it is estimated that within five years there will be Amsterdam-style coffee shops springing up all across the country. Within ten years you will be able to walk into WH Spliff or Superdrug and buy an ounce of very good skunk, or give 'shit tokens' to your friends to spend as they see fit. Within fifteen years cannabis will be made compulsory (except to firemen and nurses) and a golden new age will dawn in which we will all love each other in public places and refuse to work for more than four hours a day (one reason the firemen won't have to worry about it, seeing that's what they do already).

Admittedly, the experts who predict this are largely stoned out of their skulls and believe they will soon be taken away by a giant spaceship, but what the hell. At worst, you can tear this book into little strips and use them as roaches. It's a lot cheaper than the £10 notes cokeheads have to use. So who's laughing now, eh?

Anyway, enjoy.

VSG

Chapter 1

Potted Facts and Fallacies

Much has been written about the medical or social effects of using pot. Here are some of the more common facts and fallacies, plus a couple we made up for effect.

Facts

Pot is psychologically addictive

Genuine pot addicts know only too well how it can control their lives, interfere with their work and ruin their relationships. However, the absence of a strong chemical dependency makes it one of the easier addictions to fight. If the first thing you do in the morning is roll a blunt, it's time to wake up, smell the BO and cut down.

Fact:
Weed causes cancer

Well, yes, it does – in fact neat cannabis joints are far more dangerous than cigarettes. But given how often scientists come up with a new theory, don't be surprised to discover oxygen, water and true love are carcinogenic too.

Fact:
It keeps the Third World Third

Absolutely true. Marijuana is a hugely profitable crop, controlled by crime lords simply because it cannot be sold legitimately. Meanwhile, we're happy to let these countries grow tobacco, buy arms and enter Miss World, basically because it suits us to do so.

Fact:
It enhances creativity

Again, certainly true. Dope has been inspiring great literature (Coleridge, Baudelaire), science (Sagan, Galileo), art (Warhol, Basquiat) and music (too many to mention) for centuries. We just prefer to ignore it because we don't want little Nigel rolling a fat one while doing his homework. More's the pity.

Fact:
It kills your brain cells

Faster than Schwarzenegger with an Uzi, in fact. However, so does alcohol, boxing and watching *Fame Academy*. Given we only use 30 per cent of our brain cells anyway, who's counting? (NB: If you can't actually count any more, better cut down.)

Fallacies

Pot is chemically addictive

According to most current research, casual use of pot is no more chemically addictive than chocolate. Even the support group Marijuana Anonymous concedes 'If you haven't crossed over the line from using to abusing to addiction, you can probably quit using it any time you'd like.'

Fallacy:
Using weed will turn you onto harder drugs

A recent report by a US think-tank, the Rand Corporation, supports what potheads have been arguing for years, albeit incoherently. Cannabis is *not* a gateway drug and claiming otherwise is a bit like saying watching *Songs of Praise* will eventually turn you into a priest.

Fallacy:
Potheads resort to crime to feed their habit

Although undoubtedly true for harder drugs, there is no real evidence linking pot to street crime. A pothead is far less likely to steal your handbag than attempt to strike up a meaningful conversation with it. In fact, if you are menaced by a stoned mugger you can usually escape by throwing a Mars Bar into the path of an oncoming bus.

Fallacy:
It makes you paranoid

Again, highly debatable. Most potheads prefer not to answer the door because they don't want to be busted rather than from any deeper fear of the outside world. Also, they don't want little kids pointing and saying, 'Look, Mummy, that junkie hasn't got any trousers on!'

Fallacy:
It makes your head swell up and explode

Simply not true. This is another urban myth thought up by the CIA along with 'It turns you into a Commie' and 'It makes you sound as dumb as the President'.

Chapter 2

Laws and Legal Defences

In June 2003, cannabis will be downgraded from a Class B narcotic to a Class C. On paper, this would seem to make little difference. Smokers can still be cautioned and dealers prosecuted, so what does it really mean to the average pothead?

There are two ways to understand this; first by examining how the law will be interpreted in your area and second by understanding how drugs are categorized in the first place.

Each police authority will be free to deal with the new law in its own way. For example, in London possession may well be overlooked, whereas in Scotland it will always receive a caution and in Cornwall you will be lectured for hours by some yokel with a funny accent unless you are herding sheep, whereupon you can claim protection under by-laws governing stoned livestock. (NB: This does not mean you can dress up as a cow and claim you were only smoking your own shit, as you will then be busted under the Pantomime Act 1948.)

Despite all these changes in the law, after three cautions the police will arrest you, whereupon you will need a cast-iron legal defence. Here are a few, updated in the light of recent legal precedent, although we make no guarantees they will work.

I am a royal butler
and I demand to see
the Queen

I am a compulsive
liar and I demand to
see Jeffrey Archer

I am an England cricketer and it improves my bowling

I am a drugs czar but I have no documents to prove it

I am a committed lunatic
and I wibble wibble
wibble wibble

I am a Freemason
and your
superintendent
is my dealer

27

**I am your father, Luke –
use the Force**

**I am a hallucination.
You must be on some
really good shit**

Drug Categories

Class C

Examples: cannabis, temazepam, diazepam, marzipan, anabolic steroids.

Penalty for possession: Formal warning or imprisonment for up to two years.

Penalty for dealing: Up to five years inside.

Class B

Examples: amphetamines, codeine, Internet porn, *Big Brother Live*.

Penalty for possession: Up to five years and an unlimited fine.

Penalty for dealing: Up to fourteen years, showering with a hardened criminal of your choice.

Class A

Examples: heroin, LSD, crack, ecstasy,
Kentucky Fried Chicken.

Penalty for possession: Up to seven
years and loss of bus-driver's licence.

Penalty for dealing: Up to life
imprisonment, showering with Jeffrey
Archer.

Chapter 3

Buying

The secret to a successful habit is knowing where and how to buy. Finding a good dealer is very much like finding a good lover; both will love you unconditionally and tolerate your failings as long as you come back to them often.

In some ways a dealer is better – for instance, he never asks what you're thinking and never causes a scene if he finds you in the company of other dealers. Either way, once you have found him, never let him go. Here is some other useful information for locating and nurturing your insignificant other.

Haunts

Dealers are notoriously secretive and very few advertise in Yellow Pages (there isn't even a category for Shit Merchants – I checked!). Their usual haunts include street corners, parks and dodgy pubs where people get shot after 10 p.m. The safest bet, however, is near primary schools, where you should look out for the suspiciously sleepy lollipop lady with the dreadlocks.

Street Names

Always use street names when purchasing weed. Common examples include hash, cake, grass, doobie, Tinky Winky, La La and Po.

Weights and Measures

Although metric is the norm for coke or smack, weed is purchased by the ounce and more is usually better. The exception to this rule is when smuggling it back through foreign airports, where a suitcase full of skunk is notoriously difficult to chalk up to 'personal use'. Unless you're Liam Gallagher, of course, in which case they're so happy to see you leave they'll usually throw in free Rizlas.

Strains

In general the harder the nickname, the stronger the weed. For example, Moroccan Black is stronger than Apple White, Misty Buff or Peach Magnolia, and matt is always harder than gloss.

Terms and Conditions

Drugs are only ever sold for cash, there is no sale or return policy and showing up with a long face and a bag of grass cuttings will get you nowhere with a Trading Standards officer. In fact, my dealer wears an amusing badge that reads 'Don't ask for credit as a machete between the shoulder blades often offends'.

Decoys

Dealers will always try to fool you into buying crap instead of shit. Many is the time I wasted good money on well-disguised oregano, Oxo or henna (actually Oxo's not bad). As a guide, if it smells so bad no one in their right mind would want it even near their bloodstream, that's the stuff you should buy.

Taboos

Dealers have their own taboos. Never pretend to be a policeman or ask them what they thought of the new Darius album unless you want first-hand experience of a drive-by shooting.

The golden rule

Dealers have absolutely no honour. In fact, some have even been known to snitch on themselves to *Crimestoppers*, such is their total absence of scruples. Never part with cash before you're holding the hash and remember the golden rule: 'An ounce in your hand is worth two in his bush'.

Chapter 4

Growing

People often ask me, 'Dr G – how exactly do you grow your own weed?' To which I reply, 'Good morning, officer, thought I spotted your helmet between the window boxes!'

And, after accidentally and repeatedly falling downstairs at Scotland Yard, I refer them to the excellent Council Flat Paradise, written by my good friend Will Rogers. After further inducement (usually to my testicles), I also tell them his address, phone number and exact movements over a thirty-day period.

As Will has not been seen for a while now, I can share with you his nine-step guide to growing weed. Follow it carefully, and remember a good man is watching his back in the showers as we speak in order to bring you this information.

Step One

Pick the right seeds. You should look for a European strain which, if potted in April, should mature by late August ... give or take a police raid.

Step Two

Pick out only the brown seeds and cover with a damp tissue to germinate. If you are tempted to eat them immediately, you really need to get out more.

Step Three

Put them in little pots, transferring them to bigger ones later. As they grow, give them up to eighteen hours of light a day.

Step Four

Pot-growing teaches you a lot about feminism. The male plants flower first and, if allowed to pollinate, will reduce the potency of the female buds, so either throw them away or only plant female seeds in the first place.

Step Five

Females take between two and five months to mature and can grow to over six foot. Towards the end of the cycle, you can induce budding by reducing the light to around twelve hours a day ... which is still more than the average junkie sees in a week.

Step Six

Once buds appear, it's time for darkness. Make with the shades, and keep them somewhere the incriminating smell won't be noticed. A cupboard will do, or failing that any college dormitory.

Step Seven

When the flowers are full, start drying them. A few hours in the oven at a very low heat should do it, but be vigilant – this could be the most expensive meal you ever burned.

Step Eight

This is also the time to be especially secretive. A private stash is not something to boast about, unless you want half the world finding out, and the step up to dealing (see Chapter 9) is not to be taken lightly.

Step Nine

Enjoy! It took most of your summer and turned you into a narcoleptic Alan Titchmash, so you undoubtedly deserve it.

Chapter 5

Rolling

The fine art of rolling joints is over 4,000 years old (5,000 if you're stoned) and has a distinguished history.

The ancient Aztecs used to roll theirs in leaves, giving a pungent smell and taste which has since been lost to all but the French, who still insist on smoking Gitanes. Paper was only widely available from the late sixteenth century but soon became the chosen means of dealing with all kinds of shit.

As dope culture spread throughout England, special respect was always reserved for those who could construct very long or fat spliffs. In fact, Samuel

Pepys refers to it extensively in his diary, for example in an entry for July 1685:

"I had heard it said that the man, Winston, was a dishevelled and ill-mannered brute. However, on the occasion I met him he carried a most impressive blunt, fully 10 skins wide, which he was kind enough to share with me. After but two puffs, we were debating the merits of Ska over Lover's Rock and were totally mashed and shit-faced. Hurrah!"

Here are some of the more common or impressive joints you can roll.

The Camberwell Carrot

Immortalized in the movie *Withnail and I* as a joint consisting of twelve skins or more. Not to be confused with a Bromley-by-Bow Bean or Maida Vale Marrow.

The King Dong

An immensely long blunt that sags in the middle unless supported by an unfeasibly long roach.

The Ian Duncan-Spliff

A tiny, badly rolled joint that burns too quickly, satisfies no one and suddenly disintegrates, scorching a hole your own carpet.

The Exxon Valdez

A blunt packed with so many toxic chemicals that one puff will reduce you to the intelligence level of a very stoned moth.

The Jeffrey Archer

A pothead who claims he can roll the biggest spliffs you ever saw, before admitting he doesn't have any weed and doesn't actually smoke.

The Hindenburg

An unusually fat joint, far too wide to contain its own mass. Has a habit of collapsing when you nod off and burning your house down.

Of course, this is just a guide to get you started. The true pothead will experiment – so go to it. Invent your own weird and unfeasible construction and fill it with all manner of worthless crap – who knows, you might get a Lottery grant and P. Y. Gerbeaux to help you roll it!

Chapter 6

Smoking

Having rolled your massive doobie, you now have to smoke it correctly. Many an amateur toker has been revealed by coughing, setting fire to his clothes or generally looking like a penis.

There are basically six smoking techniques, each with its own merits and connotations. You can experiment with all of them, but best have one which you can pull off with real aplomb.

Lover's Rock

Very popular with students. As the goal here is to get another member of the group stoned and into bed with you, the spliff must be shared as often as possible. The correct way to do this is to pass it in an anti-clockwise direction, giggling, 'Is it working yet?' before falling in a heap on the floor as soon as it does.

Bob Marley

A common technique, which involves slowly taking on the mannerisms of a Jamaican as the joint is smoked. Initial drags are silent and slightly suspicious, later you begin to wheeze 'Yes, man' or 'Ai!' between puffs, smile for no apparent reason and turn up the hi-fi volume to frankly staggering levels.

Honky Toke

Hold the joint between index and middle finger, curled into the cup of your hand. This enables nervous white boys to puff away within full view of policemen, teachers or disapproving parents, as the joint can be crushed out at a moment's notice. Sadly, the other symptoms of smoking dope (such as ravenous hunger and talking crap) are not so easy to conceal.

Rude Boy

Here the joint is proudly displayed and smoked in full public view. Each drag is punctuated by a comment such as 'Jeez, this is good shit' while steadfastly refusing to pass it around. Beware of someone eventually grabbing the spliff, taking a deep draw and declaring, 'This isn't weed, you twat, it's camomile tea!'

Mr Bombastic

Easily the most popular technique as it involves rolling very large or potent joints and sharing them freely with anyone who asks. Usually reserved for dealers or growers who have lost the will to live or feel a sudden urge to be arrested.

Rastafarian

To smoke weed as Jah intended, you really have to inhale the whole blunt in one, hold it deep in your lungs and then exhale in one continuous stream of smoke. This is an advanced technique; novices will either pass out from the lack of oxygen or become so stoned that they attempt to hump fire hydrants.

Chapter 7

Eating

Of course, smoking is only one way of enjoying pot. You can freebase it (using a bong or, at a push, a teapot). You can eat it neat; as a rabbit with a death wish might. Or you can use it to make any number of tasty dishes to share with or slip to your friends.

Indeed, with the current relaxation in possession laws, we can expect see society dope-dinner parties springing up everywhere over the next few years.

To this end, I am about to publish a new cookery book called *How To Be A Domestic Junkie*, packed with tasty meals, cocktails and pictures of me looking chic in my one Metallica T-shirt and elegantly wasted underpants. Although I had no formal experience of cordon bleu I figure neither did Ainsley Harriot, so what the hell.

Anyway, here are a few recipes from the book.

Jamaican Rarebit

A bit like Welsh rarebit, only instead of cheese you use skunk. Tastes great on toast, but when you're that stoned so does everything else.

Dope Stew

Put small chunks of meat or chicken, carrots, onion and potatoes in a large pot. Add stock and season with half an ounce of finely grated dope. Cook slowly, inhaling the fumes. By the time the meat is stewed so will you be.

Corned Beef Hash

Take one tin of corned beef and one ounce of Moroccan Black. Smoke the hash, eat the corned beef and spend the rest of the evening playing strip-Twister with your guests in the living room. Your soirees will be the toast of London in no time.

Rastafarian Prawn Cocktail

Very much like ordinary prawn cocktail except you replace the lettuce with marijuana leaves. Delicious as a snack or a substitute for high tea.

Black Forest Gateau

Eat or smoke all the black first. Then sod the recipe, let's have some of that chocolate!

Sensimilia Sunrise

Take one part gin, one part Cinzano, one part orange juice and three parts pure sensi. Shake over crushed ice and serve. By the time you come round it should be nearly dawn.

Smorgasweed

A variation on the popular Swedish buffet. Different types of weed are laid out on the table for your guests to help themselves. Eventually this will provoke quite an appetite, although by this point they may have eaten the table anyway.

Chapter 8

Using

Much has been said about the long-term effects of using dope. Critics claim it causes memory loss, chronic hunger and rampant paranoia. So is it true?

To be honest, I can't remember. However, this much I do know; it's all part of a sinister conspiracy to control our every waking action ... and I'm starving!

However, using drugs is more of a lifestyle decision than a medical one. So let us examine nine things you shouldn't really do whilst using dope, and ten you can probably do better. Simply weigh up your options and make your choice. Can't say fairer than that, can we?

Shouldn't

Operate heavy machinery

Although controlling a wrecking-ball while stoned does have a certain appeal ('Hey guys, I nearly hit Parliament! Did you see?'), it will usually land you in jail.

Work for a tabloid newspaper

If you're going to make up stories for a living, might as well do it from home with a face-full of chocolate cake, eh? Wrong. Journalism usually requires you to come into work, primarily to spell-check the rumours you pinch off the Internet. Pity.

Teach

Generally, potheads make very bad teachers. Children hate sitting around for hours while you try to play 'Stairway to Heaven' on the recorder and parents resent end-of-term reports that begin 'Jemima excels in domestic science, however her hash brownies need some work.'

Become a brain surgeon

Requiring total concentration and steady hands, this is obviously beyond the skill of most potheads. Yes, even if they promise only to operate on fellow junkies, where the odd lobotomy would probably go unnoticed.

Play for the England football team

Unlike cricket, junkies would fare poorly on the soccer pitch. Fans tend to notice if you eat the missiles they throw at you or nod off during free kicks. May we recommend playing for Scotland instead?

Hold up a bank

Potheads make terrible gangsters. They can usually handle the bursting in and getting everyone up against a wall. However, at this point they have a tendency to lose interest, get the munchies or say, 'So, anyone else want to try holding the gun? It's cool!'

Become an astronaut

NASA has always had a strict policy on substance abuse, which means very few potheads ever make it into space. Mind you, as most of us have already walked on the moon, eaten powdered food straight out of the container and peed into a small bag because we couldn't be arsed to get up, who cares?

Win the Olympic 100 metres

Potheads can run fast when they need to (the sound of a police siren usually does the trick) so physical speed is not an issue. The real problem is that as soon as the starting pistol goes off, the average pothead will throw himself face down on the track screaming, 'OK, OK — I swear I'll pay you Tuesday!'

Reach the North Pole, climb Everest or cross the Sahara

Again, not so much an issue of ability as desirability. Have you any idea how hard it is to find a KFC in the Sahara??? It's bloody impossible.

Should

Become a prostitute

In most careers being barely aware of your actions is a liability. Not in this one, though.

Work at a fast-food outlet

Apart from occasionally grilling your own fingers, this is the perfect job for a pothead. Try not to eat more food than you sell.

Be a prisoner

Drugs are like a second currency in prison and if you didn't have a habit when on the way in, you probably will on the way out. They also numb the boredom, so if you intend to be a career criminal, taking drugs is just another form of share ownership.

Run for US President

Let's be honest, if you blow up the wrong country by mistake, who's going to complain? France? Oh no, I'm so scared ...

Play for the England cricket team

Seeing as they've tried everything else, flaying the bat around lethargically and lying down to stop balls seems as good a technique as any.

Be Michael Flatley

Although potheads have many limitations, dancing like a bell-end while not realizing everyone's laughing at them has never been one.

Become Pope

Sitting around all day with your head falling to one side is no problem for the average stoner. You also get to change Catholic doctrine by updating certain miracles, for instance 'The Sermon at the KFC' and the 'Turning Oregano into Sensimilia'.

Be a rock star

Although rock stars enjoy a smorgasbord of illegal drugs, learning how to play and perform used to make it a tough profession. However, since the invention of sampling, lip-syncing and boy-bands, virtually anyone with a haircut can do it. Try to find a cool name, such as Simply Dred, Boys 2 Junkies or Jefferson Shitface.

Become a TV weatherman

An exceptionally easy profession which requires little more than pointing at a map and being wrong 60 per cent of the time. If the autocue mentions the word hurricane, don't scream 'Oh no, my weeds!' and run off.

Sell the Big Issue

Looking miserable, hanging round street corners and being spurned by the general public is child's play to the average pothead. What's more, seeing as most junkies will end up doing this anyway, it's a career path with real potential.

Chapter 9

Dealing

You know how it is. You're sitting in your flat, stoned as two hippies convicted of blasphemy and running low on chocolate, when suddenly it hits you ...

'Hey, I know ... ' you say, 'why don't we mix the lighter fluid with carbonara sauce and the rest of the chocolate and ... No hang on, that's not it. Oh yes, why don't we start dealing and make a shit-load of money?'

And that's how easy it is to turn a bad habit into a crap career.

In reality, dealing is very hard work indeed, much like being an estate agent except that lying about the value of your property is not so much par for the course as a sure way of getting knifed in the back. Other than that, it's an interesting profession that guarantees your circle of friends will double overnight and continue to grow exponentially until the day you are locked up. This is generally a good thing, provided you like your friends smelly, semi-comatose and permanently hungry.

Basically, the dealing process is split into four main areas, so let's look at each area in turn ... and pass me that spliff, will you? Now where was I?

To make the perfect carbonara sauce you need the following: smoked bacon, cream, Wagon Wheels, Cheesy Wotsits ... and ...

Oh right ... sorry.

Supply

The first challenge of dealing is knowing where to get your stuff. If you can get to the top level (drug barons who import or grow their own) the stakes are very high. They will expect you to purchase loads every month and if you miss a payment you're dead. One rung lower down is the boss, usually good for a few ounces but often the first to be rolled over by the police, whereupon he will squeal like a rat at an orgy and you'll get busted too. Finally there are the street dealers, who sell too high and small for you to make any money.

The higher up the chain you go the greater the risks and the profits. Other than that, the only tip we can give you is ...

Things not to say to a drug baron

'Testing ... testing ... So, Mr dreadlock-wearing gentleman, please lean a bit closer to my lapel and say clearly how much you want for the Class-C narcotics ... man.'

Demand

Having secured your supply, it is customary to swear on your mother's bong that you will only sell it to trusted friends. Despite this, within ten hours your hallway will begin filling up with odd-looking strangers wanting a fix. Usually they claim to have heard about you from a bloke down the pub named Dougie.

Ten hours later, some of these reprobates will have moved into your living room and are refusing to leave. They eat the entire contents of your fridge, ask if they can shag your girlfriend and begin urinating on your carpet. At around the same time, you notice several overweight men are watching your house with binoculars. They claim to be bird-watchers tipped off by someone named Dougie about the presence of a golden eagle in your rafters. Shortly afterwards, you are either mugged by the strangers in your living room or arrested by the bird-watchers outside. Either way, your stash will be gone by the time you wake up.

Protection

To prevent this happening in future you will need some kind of protection. This usually involves installing a metal gate in front of your door, and buying some kind of weapon to deal with those who seem intent on ripping you off. Sadly, the presence of the gate only guarantees more bird-watchers outside, and the average gang of Yardies carrying semi-automatics and machetes are less than impressed with you waving a Swiss army knife shouting, 'Watch out, I've got a corkscrew attachment!'

Ambition

All of which leads you to the sobering conclusion that there is no such thing as an amateur dealer. You either do it properly or get used to being bothered, burgled and banged up at regular intervals for the rest of your life.

So all in all, not a great life. In fact, dealing is a bit like ...

Chapter 10

Quitting

The social pressure not to do drugs is relentless, although most of the arguments are based on prejudice or ignorance. Best be prepared with a few choice retorts, then.

Argument   Weed is approximately nine times as carcinogenic as tobacco.

Retort   So? (not a great argument, but hugely annoying to the recipient)

Argument   You have children and have
to give them a positive
image to live up to.

Retort   Parental role models are one
of the hardest things a child
has to cope with. Far better
to present an image they can
easily exceed, and what
better than a parent who sits
around on his arse all day
eating chocolate?

Argument   You have begun to lose your short-term memory.

Retort   If you're over forty, you've only got ten years of good memory and controllable body functions anyway.

Argument You begin to fear the world is out to get you.

Retort It is, get over it.

Argument You have begun to lose your short-term memory.

Retort Er ... what was the question again?

Argument You become uncontrollably lethargic and complacent, your friends find you boring and your employer wants to sack you.

Retort Yeah, whatever ...

Argument   You can no longer afford to feed your habit.

Retort   Sell something unnecessary. I mean, do you really need a stove when you've already got a perfectly good toaster?

Argument   You are experiencing sexual problems, and marijuana is a known cause of impotency.

Retort   You're over thirty and have been with the same partner for ages — you're lucky to be using your penis at all.

Argument You have lost all interest in current popular music.

Retort Great music ended in the late 60s anyway. What you gonna enjoy instead? Westlife? I think not.

Argument The water company cut off
your supply months ago.

Retort Washing is bad for you, man.
I heard it on the Internet.

However, despite such irrefutable logic, all good things must end and quitting is something most of us consider from time to time. At this point you will discover some unexpectedly hard truths.

1) That cannabis is not such a soft drug and is definitely not easy to give up. Be prepared for mood swings, chronic boredom and the realization that daylight is not necessarily your enemy. On the plus side, you will notice that you can do a lot more in the average day than listen to the same album over and over again.

2) That you miss your girlfriend, whom you hadn't noticed walking out about six months previously. There are many ways to win back an ex-partner, but saying 'I've quit dope, wash regularly and can now conduct a proper conversation' is more persuasive than most.

3) That Kentucky Fried Chicken is not quite as delicious as it appeared while stoned. Furthermore, eating it three times a day makes you fart, and now that your sense of smell has returned it's not pleasant.

4) That you can now afford to reclaim some of your possessions and the cashpoint no longer seems to laugh sarcastically when you try to take money out.

5) That it's a cold, unfriendly world out there, full of crap music and complex relationships, and without dope to give it a warm fuzzy edge, life looks very scary indeed. Get used to it.

So quit or don't, it's up to you, but don't come crying to me when the bailiffs call or you're left with nothing to shag but the cat. Remember the cosmic truth of all substance abuse:

'Tis better to have used and quit, than never to have used at all.'

About the Author

V. S. Ganjabhang comes from a large family of Dutch origin which has been slowly moving northwards under the cover of elm disease. Despite an Oxford education, he abandoned a promising career in animal psychology after sharing a joint with the Best of Breed winner at Crufts in 1982. Since then he has become a well-known pundit on the subject of drugs, fighting a heroic defence against media sensationalism.

'I'm not saying that tabloid newspapers are a bigger danger to society than drug barons,' he said in 1998, 'but no drug baron ever photographed my mum in a compromising position with a horse, did they? I rest my case.'

Ganjabhang is single, which comes as a surprise to no one. He wishes to thank Will Rogers, Jasmine Birtles and Guillaume Mutsaars, without whose help he wouldn't be in this mess.